A WHOLE LANGUAGE PRIMER*

*(MOST LIKELY AN OXYMORON)

Lee Gunderson

SCHOLASTIC

Scholastic-TAB Publications Ltd.
123 Newkirk Road, Richmond Hill, Ontario, Canada L4C 3G5

Scholastic Inc.
730 Broadway, New York, NY 10003, USA

Ashton Scholastic Pty Limited
PO Box 579, Gosford, NSW 2250, Australia

Ashton Scholastic Limited
165 Marua Road, Panmure, Auckland 6, New Zealand

Scholastic Publications Ltd.
Holly Walk, Leamington Spa, Warwickshire CV32 4LS, England

Cover by Willem Hart
Author photo by Martin Dee, Jr.

ISBN 0-590-73295-1

10 9 8 7 6 5 4 3 2   Printed in USA   0 1 2 3 4 5/9

INTRODUCTION

Thousands of teachers across North America have adopted and adapted something called whole language as a philosophical base (see *whole language philosophy*) to support the particular form of literacy learning environment (see *high literacy environment*) they have chosen to create in their classrooms. No other approach to teaching has produced such dedicated disciples and advocates. Indeed, they feel a great sense of *ownership* (see also *empowerment*) — as well they might, since they are the inventors not only of the approaches themselves but also of the special vocabulary that accompanies them.

This *Primer* is dedicated to all those teachers who have made whole language an important means to literacy learning. It presents whole language vocabulary and terms that have been observed in use in classrooms and conferences across North America. To some it will serve as an introduction to the world of the whole language classroom. To others it will serve as a sourcebook of varying perspectives of whole language. Some references, such as *ownership* above, are printed in heavy italic type; you will find an entry for those terms elsewhere in the text.

The *Primer* is based on observations of, and conversations with, whole language teachers from across the continent. It does not contain every item of whole language vocabulary, because that vocabulary is constantly expanding; the complete whole language terminology has not yet been invented, nor is there even universal agreement about the terms that *do* exist. For instance, some items may seem to you inaccurate, because they represent someone's particular definition, developed independently. If so, I urge you to write to me with a definition of your own, or with a new vocabulary item you think should be included. (You will find a Contributor's Form at the end of the *Primer* which you may photocopy to submit your suggestions.) Perhaps you will be cited in a future edition. At least, you will receive a certificate of appreciation, suitable for framing, boldly adorned with either a gold or a silver star.

And now, *A Whole Language Primer*.

A-a

affective components — Many students do not like school, and never will. Most dropouts, especially boys, do not look back with great affection to the hours spent sitting on hard wooden chairs listening to teachers talking about reading and writing. Sometimes, though, negative attitudes can be more subtle. In a series of studies, Jon Shapiro found that *literature-based programs* produced more boys who considered reading an appropriate activity for them than did *skills-based instruction*. The girls' attitudes towards reading, unlike the boys', did not appear to be affected by the type of classroom in which they read. Is it possible that, when we use *traditional teaching* methods, we are instilling in boys an aversion to reading and language arts?

aide — Often referred to as a para-professional, an aide helps the teacher with the instructional program. Most often, whole language aides are involved in helping students write and record their writing, usually in the *publishing* center. The province of Manitoba has changed the term *classroom aides* to the potentially less offensive *classroom assistants*.

almost whole language — A pejorative phrase referring to the classrooms and/or programs of teachers who don't understand the whole language approach. "I do whole language for fifteen minutes of the reading period and then use the basals because my students can't really do without them." (A teacher from Thunder Bay, overheard in Toronto) Such an individual is referred to as an "almost whole language" teacher. (See also *part language*.)

apple — Normally a gift for the teacher. Today, however, the Apple is a *computer* used in the classroom for games, classroom *management* and, especially, word processing. (See also *FrEd Writer*.)

assessment — Whole language teachers and their principals are very often confronted by parents who want to know how their children's learning is to be assessed. Administrators, especially, look nervously and with apprehension at classrooms where students do not fill out worksheets and workbooks. Often, whole language teachers become refuseniks. Since they believe standardized tests are inadequate measurements of literacy in a *holistic* environment, they refuse to administer them. Assessments such as the *cloze* procedure are preferred, because they use connected discourse and do not focus on isolated skills.

attitudes — The right attitudes (or "tudes") are vital to learning. Whole language involves students in activities they enjoy. "Motivation is high, students have all the right 'tudes." (Heard in San Francisco.) See *affective components* for a reference to whole language and male-female reading attitudes.

audience — The person or persons for whom a communication is intended, often called the *intended audience*. Whole language teachers believe students should read and write for someone real rather than for someone imaginary or invented — or for the usual audience understood by students, namely the teacher. (See also *real audience*.)

B-b

basal bashing — Some reading researchers regularly condemn *basal readers* as the source of a great number of problems students encounter in learning to read. Such condemnation is referred to as basal bashing. (Contributed by Dr. Richard McCallum of the University of California at Berkeley.)

basalese — A term referring to the speech contained in *basal readers*. Basalese contains repetitive vocabulary and simple syntactic patterns such as: *See Dick run. Run, Dick, run. Run, run, run.* (See *book talk, talk, talk.*) Whole language teachers find such texts reprehensible.

basalitis — Some students come to dislike reading because of the constant drudgery of workbook activities, and these poor unfortunates are said to have developed basalitis. "He's been filling out workbooks for so long he's got basalitis." (Heard in Vancouver.)

basalized — Students who have been taught reading through the use of *basals* are often said to have been basalized. Some basalized students seem to enjoy filling in worksheets and answering multiple choice questions. Nevertheless, the term is considered pejorative.

basals, basal readers — Published reading programs designed to present the thousands of *skills* thought to be important in learning to read. The skills are usually noted on a *scope and sequence* chart. Basal reading programs are organized around basal reading texts, which are sequenced according to level of difficulty. Basal readers are criticized because they contain repetitious and "unreal" language. Some publishers have begun to market *whole language basals*, anathema to the true believer but comforting to the neophyte whose principal insists that he or she "do whole language."

bibliography — A list of authors and their publications, the inclusion of which, in an article or book, purports to add authority thereto. The possession of a good (that is to say a big) bibliography is important, because it demonstrates to the reader that others support what the author is saying. In a recent letter to the editor of *The Vancouver Sun*, a writer suggested that whole language was well researched (see *research*), because he had read a chapter in a book that had over 100 items in its bibliography! The value of bibliographies is clear: with them, professors publish; without them, they perish.

big books — Big books are large-format books published either by students in a classroom or by a publishing company. The concept of the big book is not a new one. The classic big book, written by William S. Gray and published in 1951 by Scott Foresman, was titled *Our Big Book* and contained the familiar tales of Dick and Jane. Nowadays, students produce their own big books by contributing stories on themes (see *theme books*), which the teacher then collates and publishes. Whole language teachers use big books for reading activities, to encourage *chiming in* and choral reading. Big books are also published in miniature, for students to have their own small-size versions of the story.

book talk — Book talk differs from real language because it contains many writing conventions. Some whole language teachers strive to show their students that this is so. (See also *talk talk*) Book talk contains complete sentences, complex syntactic structures, mature spelling, and standardized punctuation — unless, of course, it happens to be *basalese*, the stilted and mangled language peculiar to *basal readers*, which differs from both.

brainstorming — Students work together, as a class or in small groups, to develop lists of ideas or statements about particular subjects. They may be asked, for instance, to generate lists of items related to pollution just before reading an article on the subject. From brainstorming flow *prediction* activities that foster higher levels of comprehension of content-area texts, such as science and social studies.

buddy, buddies — A pairing of students, usually an older one paired with a younger. For example, a writing buddy in a higher grade provides a *real audience*, rather than a pretend one, for a young writer. Computer networking (see *networking, poor man's networking*) allows students to develop writing buddies over great distances, even from other countries.

burnout — Whole language programs require a prodigious amount of planning and teacher-student contact time. As a result, whole language teachers are often concerned about becoming "burned out" and frequently form *support groups* in order to help each other face the bracing rigors of the whole language classroom. They are convinced, however, that the joy they derive from seeing their students develop more than makes up for all the time and energy the program requires. They also witness their students' joy, which results from positive attitudes towards literacy activities. As a general rule, teachers who use *basals* are denied this privilege, since they do not normally see students becoming either excited or joyful when they fill in workbooks.

busy time — A period in whole language classrooms when students should all be working on "something they want to or have to get done." Busy time is usually not a particularly quiet time, since students use it to discuss their work with each other. In some classes, busy time is also supposed to be *quiet time*. In general, however, whole language teachers differentiate between busy time, which can be loud, and quiet time, when students are asked to work quietly on reading or writing. (See also *uninterrupted sustained silent reading, uninterrupted sustained silent reading or writing*, and *uninterrupted sustained silent writing*.) In basal classrooms, busy time is usually "make work" time, a gradgrindish interlude of utterly useless and pointless filling in of workbooks and worksheets, the educational equivalent of picking oakum.

C-c

centers (**centres** elsewhere in the world) — Whole language students are given a great deal of choice in learning, often through a wide variety of learning centers (sometimes called *stations*) where they can learn independently. This concept is borrowed from the "individualized education" concepts of the past (see *individualization*).

chanting — Some whole language teachers believe that students should be encouraged to learn reading by chanting stories and poems together. Students enjoy this activity, particularly readers who are still unsure of their ability, since no one individual is singled out during chanting. Some whole language teachers believe that learning to chant a text helps students acquire the phrasing that will enable them to become good readers, but others believe that chanting is not very productive, since it does not seem particularly meaningful (see *meaningful learning*). "He's been chanting for three years, but doesn't yet understand what he's chanting." (Heard in Toronto.) Occasionally chanting is accompanied by clapping.

child, children — Terms used by primary teachers to refer to *students*. One can differentiate between primary teachers and teachers of older students by phrases such as: "My children are working on a project" versus: "My students are working on a project." Vice-principals remain impartial on this issue. Under stress, they refer to both groups as pains in the ___.

chiming in — Many whole language teachers believe that students learn when they are provided with a positive model to emulate. As the teacher reads text aloud, often from a *big book*, students are encouraged to "chime in" and read aloud with the teacher, thereby emulating a good oral reading model. (See also *chanting, choral reading*.)

choral reading — An activity in which a whole class reads a whole story aloud. Many whole language teachers believe choral reading is a good method for helping students to develop good phrasing, stress, and intonation. Choral reading is related to *chiming in*, *chanting*, and *jazzing*.

chunking — A term used in psychology to explain a human being's ability to remember more when items are grouped than when they are isolated. For example, it's easier to remember *1989* than *one, nine, eight, nine*. Whole language teachers usually employ the term in reference to the study of novels. In this case, it is easier for students to derive meaning, and therefore enjoyment, from a novel if they chunk it into chapters rather than dissecting each sentence in an effort to squeeze every scintilla of meaning from it.

class library, classroom library — A mini-library, selected by the teacher to meet the needs and interests of the students, contained in the classroom and often located in the reading *center*. Teachers discover the students' interests by administering oral or written *interest inventories*.

cloze: testing — The usual procedure for finding books which students can read and from which they can learn is to give a test. However, whole language teachers abhor tests, since they focus attention on skills, such as the decoding of nonsense syllables. They feel that in order to measure how well a student can read a particular book they should test the student with real material from the book itself. The best method, according to many teachers, is to give students a selection of about 250 words from which they have systematically eliminated perhaps every fifth word. The students then supply the deleted words. This is known as the cloze procedure, which William Taylor suggested in 1953 as a good measure of comprehension, and which has been shown to be a useful device for matching students with text. Teachers like it because it puts students in contact with the actual language of the text. Unfortunately, there is little agreement on what cloze scores really mean. See Bormuth for a discussion of this question.

cloze: scoring — Cloze can test three comprehension levels: independent, instructional, and frustration. A student operating at the independent level is able to comprehend the text and needs no help from the teacher. At the instructional level, the ideal level from a teaching point of view, the teacher will have to provide help. At the frustration level, no amount of help will suffice to enable the student to comprehend the text — it is simply too difficult. There is almost no agreement on what scores mean, however, with different authors recommending such widely different scoring criteria that one researcher's frustration level becomes another's instructional level. Bormuth's scoring criteria (1967) are widely used.

cloze: teaching — Whole language teachers believe ***prediction*** is an important part of reading, and cloze teaching requires students to make predictions. This is one way of doing it: A passage from a book is read aloud, with one word in every 10 or 15 omitted. By using a gesture of some kind, the teacher cues students to fill in, orally, the missing word. If students are given printed text, then the omissions are signaled by blanks in the text. To fill in the missing words, students have to focus on context rather than on letter-sound correspondences or spelling patterns.

committees — Students are often asked to form groups to work together on projects. Teachers form committees for specific purposes. Teachers also serve on committees: "He's put me on the social committee again." "Well that's better than the coffee committee for five years." (Heard in Seattle.) One large secondary school, the exact location of which, for obvious reasons, I shall refrain from revealing, has a multiplicity of committees. Among their number is one whose sole purpose is to keep track of all the other committees to ensure that no committee ends up doing nothing!

compatibility — A term frequently used in reference to computers. A program designed for one computer can only be used on other computers if they are compatible. Most often teachers find that the three computers they bought with the money their class made on a paper drive are not compatible.

comprehension — The obvious goal of all reading/language arts programs is to develop students' abilities to understand material they read or hear. Generally, comprehension is categorized into three or four levels; literal, inferential, and critical/evaluative. Because literal comprehension leaves students' attention on the surface structure of a text and not on its meaning, it should be emphasized less than the other two. (See also ***reading***, ***DRTA***.) One important component of comprehension is ***prediction***. There would be widespread agreement in the prediction of the missing word in: "He's a blithering ____." In fact, this simple sentence can be a rather effective measure of students' English ability. A student of English as a Second Language (ESL) might predict "boy," because he thinks about English syntax and predicts an animate noun. Native English speakers, on the other hand, would predict "fool" or "idiot," since both are semantically co-constrained and learned through experience. ***Cloze*** is based on our ability to predict as we read.

computer, microcomputer — The computer has become a desired teaching aid, serving as: a record keeper for teachers, an entertainment center featuring games to keep students busy, an ***electronic workbook***, and a word processor and publishing unit. Buying computers is always a major effort for schools and school districts, which often fund the purchases by having bake sales. A single school may have five different kinds of computers — which causes some difficulty in the area of ***compatibility***.

conference — The whole language approach requires that students and teachers communicate, through group conferences and individual student-teacher conferences in which the student reports personal progress and the teacher asks questions, probes, and suggests further development. There are several kinds of conferences:

- *Writing conference* — In whole language classrooms, students are asked to write often and in various forms (see *writing development*). The teacher reads their writing and composes messages in reply. Teachers *never* correct students' writing in the traditional sense, but do make positive comments about both the content and the form.

- *Reading conference* — The teacher meets with students to discuss and record their progress, often taking notes in a ***conference log***.

- *Group interest conference* — Whole language teachers often form groups around students' interests. A teacher might have a conference

   with the "science fiction" group, for instance. (See ***interest inventories***.)

conference log — The conference log is a record of the student's progress and the teacher's suggestions, discussed during a ***conference***. The information on conference logs can be used to group students if the teacher believes in either ***inductive*** or ***deductive teaching***. A typical conference log (see next page) gives an overview of the student's progress, needs, and interests. This sample log refers only to reading, but it could also contain information about writing, an especially important feature of the whole language classroom.

D-d

DRTA — Directed reading-thinking activity, an activity that promotes students' prediction during reading, first suggested by Stauffer in 1971. In 1983, I described a version of DRTA that involved students in first reading portions of a story and then predicting what would happen.

deductive teaching — A teaching activity in which students are presented with facts in a lecture, and are responsible for "receiving the truths" told to them. Whole language teachers generally disagree with this approach, because the learning is not meaningful. It is directed by the teacher, who has selected the material to be learned and who is in charge of the learning, rather than by the students.

direct instruction — Many teachers believe that there are certain *skills* students need to learn before they can become successful readers, and that these skills are best taught directly. For example, a teacher who believes that learning *phonics* is important will directly teach phonic relationships. Whole language teachers generally believe that direct instruction is inappropriate. However, there are several shades of belief on this subject, and these result in differing nuances in teaching. (See also *instruction*.)

Many whole language teachers believe in *inductive teaching*. The inductive school of thought maintains that students should learn skills and that instruction should include the modeling of such skills as handwriting. These teachers are uncomfortable with allowing complete independence. If they find that similar *invented spelling* occurs across a group of students, for instance, they may call those students together and suggest that the time has come to do some group work.

"I am thinking of a word that begins with the sound of *ch*. Who can write a word containing the *ch* sound?" (Students write their words individually, on their papers.) "I like Sandra's word *chukul*. If you see the word *chuckle* in a book, it will look like this." (Teacher writes selected words on the chalkboard.)

As the lesson continues, the teacher attempts to have the students learn the skill inductively. The words are then used by the students in some way, perhaps in writing stories containing as many words as possible with the *ch* sound. These stories may be put into a *big book* and read by other students as part of the reading program.

Just as many whole language teachers, on the other hand, are convinced that students will learn skills on their own, independently, if they are involved in *meaningful learning* and meaningful activities. The independent school of thought maintains that no direct instruction should ever take place. Students will learn things like *phonics*, for instance, if they are given good literature and suitable oral reading models.

draft books — In some whole language classrooms, students are given draft books in which to write assigned or thematic material. The students know that the material in the draft book will be edited (see *editing*) and perfected for publication (see *writing process*). In a study that Shapiro and I conducted in 1988, we found that students began to manage draft book exercises as early as November of the first grade.

drama — Students in whole language classrooms are often involved in activities in which they assume roles and produce stories or plays. Using role playing to act out real situations is a good method for developing better understanding of real life situations. (See *role playing*.)

dreamin', dreaming — To initiate some writing activities, many whole language teachers ask students to begin by "dreamin'" in order to picture in their minds characters, descriptions, and actions. Often a dreaming activity begins the *uninterrupted sustained silent*

writing period. It is also referred to as "visualizing" or "imagining movies in your head."

drill and kill — Many authors have been cited for this phrase. I first heard it at a conference for English as a Second Language (ESL) teachers held in the state of Washington in 1983. Stephen Krashen used the phrase to describe workbook activities that require students "to fill in answers mindlessly" with little regard for the meaning of the text.

E-e

editing — Teachers who believe in writing activities ask their students to edit and, in some cases, to rewrite. Whole language teachers are careful to make editing meaningful. If not carefully controlled, editing can become a laborious chore that students grow to dread and, ultimately, to hate. They thereby also learn to hate writing. (See ***writing process***.)

electronic mail — A message communicated via a computer over telephone lines. Electronic mail allows ***networking*** over great distances. Many networks are available for electronic mail; for example, many of the secondary schools in British Columbia can communicate with other schools throughout the province. (See also ***poor man's networking***.)

electronic workbook — Many whole language teachers view the computer with a great deal of scorn because they believe it has, in most cases, simply been used as an electronic workbook. Students sit and answer questions, filling in words and letters just as they do in workbooks, and learn and profit just as little from the dreary exercise. Some teachers are especially horrified by the "rewards" students are given for getting the right answers. "Can you believe that program actually shows an airplane being shot down every time a student pushes the right letter!" (Heard in Vancouver.)

emergent literacy — Some children learn to read and write before they enter primary school, and people studying these students refer to that learning as "emergent literacy," since it seems to emerge independently, without ever having been taught. These lucky children usually come from homes where reading and writing are highly valued, homes that create what is called a **_high literacy environment_**. It is the aim of whole language teachers to emulate that sort of an environment in their classrooms. The **_research_** support for **_whole language instruction_** is mostly based on emergent literacy findings, since little research has been conducted studying whole language in classrooms.

empower, empowerment — In most schools, students do what the teachers tell them to do, and teachers do what the principal tells _them_ to do. In the case of traditional teachers, the principal generally instructs them to teach from basal readers. Whole language teachers believe they should be free to make instructional decisions based on their students' needs and interests. More than that, it is their responsibility to do so. Because they feel empowered, they are willing to ignore officially mandated **_scope and sequence_** skills teaching. In the same spirit, whole language teachers empower their students by giving them the responsibility of managing their own learning.

enemy — A term usually referring to professors for whom many whole language teachers feel a not inconsiderable degree of contempt. "The politics of the situation is that you are the enemy, trying to impose your ideas from outside the classroom. Change only takes place when we teachers take our classrooms and programs into our own hands." (Comment made to a professor of education by an avowed **_TOWL_** in Philadelphia — in fact, I was that professor.)

enemy territory — A term describing the classrooms of the non-whole language teachers in a school. Whole language classrooms encourage a great deal of student talk, which is often perceived by other teachers as "noise." "I've been getting a lot of static from enemy territory about my students talking in the library." (Heard in Calgary.) Both whole language and traditional teachers refer to each other as **_they_** or **_them_** or **_one of them_**.)

environmental print — We live in a world filled with print. Early readers quickly begin to recognize and understand the meaning of such things as stop signs, the name on the wrapper of their favorite candy bar, and the McDonald's golden arches (see **_logos_**). Whole language advocates believe the ability to "read" environmental print is a precursor to learning to read standard print. Environmental print, usually capital letters, is an important part of many whole language classrooms, where teachers use it as reading material.

errors — Whole language teachers do not believe students make errors. They do, however, make oral *miscues* in reading and use *invented spelling* in writing. Students' work is never corrected in the traditional fashion, since the red marks indicating errors are seen as discouraging for students anxious to improve. It is vitally important for whole language teachers to describe their philosophy to parents, principals, and other teachers, so that "uncorrected" papers are not viewed as a sign that the teacher does not bother to check work. (See *whole language philosophy*.) "That whole language teacher never corrects her students' work." (Heard in Abbotsford.)

experiential — Many individuals, especially professors in disciplines other than language arts and reading, are uncomfortable with the term *whole language*. They often prefer, instead, to use the word *experiential* to refer to whole language programs, since students are involved in activities in which they have experience with language. (See *reading-writing-thinking approach*, *schema theory*.)

explicit modeling — Some whole language teachers believe that explicit modeling is an important pedagogical approach, and they provide good models by letting their students hear them read and see them write. They also write, on the students' writing, comments that contain the essence of what the students indicate they have written, to give an explicit writing model. For instance, when a child writes: *ILMkBs*, and reads: "I love my Care Bears," the teacher responds in writing: *I'm glad you love your Care Bears, (name)*. In this case the teacher is explicitly modeling writing. Other whole language teachers believe explicit modeling "imposes" a correct model on students and has a negative effect. (See also *implicit modeling*, *instruction*.)

F-f

files — Students' writing is often produced on a word processor, where it is kept in files. "Have you worked on your files today?" (Heard in Kellogg.) It is important to keep students' files straight and in order.

flippers — Short, student-produced texts that students "flip" through as they read them. Flippers are stapled at the top so that the pages can be fanned. Some flippers have illustrations only, and when the pages are flipped, the illustrations seem to move.

FrEd Writer — A simple word processing program designed for Apple computers, the *Free Educational Writer* is in the public domain and can be copied for use in classrooms.

G-g

grade — A mark used to evaluate a student's progress. Whole language teachers generally believe that grades are not useful for indicating student growth, and try to avoid giving them. Instead, they keep anecdotal records about their students' performance, as well as samples of their work, which they share with parents in order to demonstrate the students' progress. An anecdotal record might read like this: *January 8. Sheila wrote a story today in which, for the first time, she correctly spelled "happiness" and "Care Bears." Her story was well formed, with a beginning, a middle, and an end. She wrote about 200 words.* (See also *grading*.)

grading — Primary whole language teachers usually do not grade their students. Instead, they send anecdotal notes home to parents (see *grade*). Intermediate teachers express a great deal of concern about grading because they feel that they are constrained by report cards. One of the most important questions in an intermediate teacher's mind is: "How do I grade my students if I become a whole language teacher?" (Heard in Edmonton.)

graphemes — Visual symbols that represent *phonemes*, the significant speech sounds of a language, or *morphemes*, units of meaning. The grapheme *S*, for instance, normally represents the phoneme /s/, heard at the beginning of the word *sun*. The "plus" sign (+) is an example of a grapheme that represents a morpheme. *Logos* may also represent words, or series of words: *IBM* is both a logo and an acronym. *Phonics* is the study of the relationships between graphemes and phonemes. Many whole language teachers believe that teaching phonics focuses students' attention on the surface structure of a text and away from meaning.

groupies — A pejorative term referring to the apparent tendency of whole language teachers to stick together in schools and, even more, at conferences. "I just ran into some whole language groupies." (Heard in Philadelphia) (See also *support groups*.)

grouping — The idea of grouping students for instruction is anathema to some whole language teachers, who believe in whole-class instruction. However, some do group on the basis of interest.

H-h

handwriting — Generally, whole language teachers do not teach students handwriting, preferring instead that they learn how to write independently. Some, however, believe students should be guided in learning to write. (See *instruction*.)

high literacy environment — A term describing a home or classroom in which literacy activities are perceived by all as important and enjoyable. (See also *print rich environment*.)

holistic — A word describing the tendency of human beings to perceive the world in meaningful, general *patterns* rather than in individual features. It is thought that teaching and learning should be holistic, focusing on whole stories, for instance, rather than on minor features such as phonics skills. Whole language teachers often prefer the term *wholistic*.

I-i

imagining — Students are taught to make images in their head before they begin to write. Imagining is important to the writing process. (See *dreamin'*.)

implicit modeling — Some whole language teachers are convinced that students can learn to read and write independently. They therefore involve them in many print activities, including the reading of many books. They never, however, impose the mature model of writing by actually writing comments on their students' papers. All communications about writing are oral, so as not to inhibit students' natural, independent *writing development*. The "never write on students' writing" faction is appalled by the very suggestion that teachers should make written comments because, they believe, it makes the students despair that their writing is not up to standard. Some teachers are a bit more relaxed about it. The difference between these two viewpoints may seem trivial, but each side is ready, at times, to believe the worst about its opponents. (See also *instruction*.)

individualization — During the 1960's, individualized instruction became quite popular. Students were allowed to work independently at their own levels. Many whole language teachers, especially those at the intermediate level, find that individualized instruction quickly becomes a feature of their programs, too. Individualized instruction requires *conferences* and classroom *management*. Some primary whole language teachers disagree, stating that they teach only whole classes and do not group students in any way, even individually. Some whole language teachers, especially the intermediate ones, have begun to look again with fondness at *SRA* kits, which are really just boxes filled with reading activities.

inductive teaching — Teaching in this way means that students are *guided* into a learning situation. The teacher does not lecture, but helps students come to learn on their own with such questions as: "Who knows how to spell . . . ?" (See also *direct instruction, instruction*.)

informal reading inventory — A form of assessment used to determine students' reading abilities. The informal reading inventory determines comprehension levels, and is favored by whole language teachers.

instruction — One of the most contentious issues in whole language today is that of instruction, upon which even whole language teachers are in disagreement. The traditional sequence of language arts learning and, hence, language arts teaching has been speaking, listening, reading, then finally writing. As a result, it has been thought that students must become readers *before* they become writers. Generally, whole language teachers, based on their interpretation of *emergent literacy* research, believe that all language arts abilities are *interactive* and develop simultaneously. They ask students to read and write from their first day of school. Students attempt to write when asked, and are able to produce text which is syntactically very complex (see *writing development*). Contention revolves around the teacher's role and, as a result, two different approaches are found in whole language classrooms:

- *Independent* — Teachers in independent classrooms are convinced that *emergent literacy research* shows that students should be allowed to develop their writing *skills* with complete independence, and that the mastery of these skills will emerge as a natural consequence of being involved in activities that are interesting and meaningful. These teachers invite students to write, encouraging those who cannot or will not, but never showing them *how* to do it. They believe in the importance of *implicit modeling*, and their classrooms are filled with writing and literature. They also believe that writing on students' writing "imposes" mature written *models*, making students feel that their writing is somehow inferior. The students display their writing everywhere in the classroom, and they read and chime in when the teacher reads. In this way they learn that print represents language and has meaning. They are given writing models, but in an implicit fashion.

- *Guided* — Teachers who believe in *explicit modeling* do not believe that a student's *writing development* is interfered with by seeing a teacher's correct *models*. They do not correct students' writing; instead, they make positive comments containing the essence of what the students say they have written. These teachers begin the year by inviting their students to write, and to this invitation the students respond in one of three different ways:

  1. They indicate that they are unable to write. The teacher then asks what they would *like* to write if they were able to do so, and writes what they say they would like to write. This is a *language experience approach* to writing.

  2. They produce picture or letter strings, which they read to the teacher. The teacher then writes responses, which convey the essence of what the students have written. For example, Shapiro and I (1988) describe the student who wrote: *eYbDksrhftft*, which he read to the teacher as: "The robots are fighting." His teacher responded, *I hope the robots don't get injured in the fight.* In this fashion the teacher provided an explicit model of the mature writing form without "imposing" it on the student.

3. They produce text with recognizable words. The teacher then writes a reply containing the essence of what the student has written.

These two schools of whole language thought seem mutually exclusive, since each group believes the worst about the other. Members of both groups are often heard volubly and intemperately criticizing those who do not subscribe to their creed. But, while the classrooms of members of these two groups will differ in dramatic and significant ways, on one point they do appear to be in agreement: both are equally negative about traditional tests, measurement, and *assessment*.

integrated learning, integrated teaching — Programs in *traditional classrooms* isolate the learning of discrete components. Students learn, and are therefore taught, spelling, handwriting, reading, oral language, and all the other important *skills*. Integrated learning views teaching and learning as integrated. One can learn science, for example, while also learning reading. The school day is not divided into separate periods during which students are taught particular skills. In 1966 the superintendent of the San Francisco Public Schools gave a presentation to the local Rotary Club. During his speech he glanced at his watch and is reported to have said: "It's 10:10. All of our elementary students have just taken out their spelling books." Whole language teachers believe that such compartmentalization is anathema to *holistic* learning.

interactive — The interactive view of reading postulates that readers use information both from the text itself and from their background knowledge to read and comprehend text. Many individuals, who want to avoid any connection with the whole language movement because of its political associations, employ the term to show that they understand its basic concept. "I'm not a whole language person, but I've been doing interactive reading programs for years." (Heard in Vancouver.)

interest group — Whole language teachers who view grouping as positive often organize groups around interests, using an *interest inventories* to identify and group students. (See also *grouping*.)

interest inventories — An instrument for discovering students' interests so the teacher may better plan their reading and writing programs. An oral inventory is extremely flexible, with the teacher simply asking the students what they enjoy reading and writing. During the session the teacher makes categories and keeps a written tally.

	Ghosts	Adventure	Science Fiction	Young Womens'
		Reading Interest Inventory		
James		x		
Francis			x	
William			x	
Andrea	x			
Mary				x
Martin		x		

Interest inventories are usually more helpful to intermediate than to primary teachers. Interest grouping is a powerful technique for teachers who believe in group **instruction**, and it is also a powerful tool for the teacher who wants to provide appropriate materials for students' independent learning.

invented spelling — Whole language teachers, recognizing that the meaning of a piece of writing is far more important than any surface structure errors, believe that students should be allowed to experiment freely with print. The students' own invented spellings, far from being "wrong," reveal their developing understanding of **phonics**. In our 1988 study, Shapiro and I found that the students' writing revealed that they were learning the rule-governed nature of phoneme/grapheme correspondences, and not randomly producing errors. On the next page is a list of invented spellings from an English as a Second Language (ESL) student in a whole language classroom. These invented spellings show that the student is learning phonic relationships. However, he overgeneralizes. For instance, the word *cride* reveals that he understands a very common **phonic generalization**, but that he has overgeneralized the relationship to an irregular spelling pattern. This is very much like the child at three saying: "I goed to the park." Rather than indicate a problem in language development, it reveals that the child is learning that language (in this case spelling) is rule governed. This is a natural and wonderful development and should be encouraged.

Invented Spelling Test

gambold	liv	ingerd	eckwotek
inglin	anesang	lisins	posativly
biring	lickores	cride	milinyer
boem	melowdi	bof	mawtans
nabors	orfenig	dropt	wrelaks

Answers: gambled, England, bring, bomb, neighbors, live, anything, licorice, melody, orphanage, injured, listens, cried, both, dropped, aquatic, positively, millionaire, mountains, relax.

J-j

jazzing — Sometimes used in place of *chanting* when students are chanting rhythmically. Jazzing is valued by some whole language teachers because they think that it helps students develop phrasing and improves their reading of text, especially narrative.

K-k

key words — Students often ask teachers how to spell certain words. Some whole language teachers write these words on flashcards and give them to the students, and they become those students' key words. (See also *personal dictionaries, word walls.*)

kill, killing — Causing a teacher great stress: "Having 35 students in my class is killing." (Heard in Toronto.) Or, a term used to mean "causing a student to become bored and uninterested," as in "Workbooks are sure kill on students." (Heard in Calgary.)

L-l

language experience approach (LEA) — In a language experience approach, students are asked about experiences they have had, and the teacher helps individuals or groups by leading a discussion and transcribing text into written form. The resulting LEA stories become part of the students' reading program. Many whole language teachers do not believe LEA should be part of students' activities because it focuses their attention on the teacher as leader of the discussion and writer of the stories. They believe that students can learn to write totally independently. Others simply use LEA to help students begin writing when they first enter school, abandoning it later. (See *instruction*, *explicit modeling*.)

libraries, librarians — The school library and the school librarian are the whole language teacher's best friends. They provide sources for the *classroom library*, for collections of books related to students' interests, and for the good children's literature that should be used to help students learn to read.

literature — Whole language teachers believe that real literature should be used as part of the instructional program. Good literature uses more natural language than *basal readers*. It is therefore easier for students to understand and, as a result, proves of greater interest to them.

literature-based — Some whole language teachers design their programs around literature, in the belief that students can come to learn to read by being exposed to hearing and reading good literature.

logos — Logos represent companies and services, and are one of the first kinds of environmental print that children are able to "read and understand." Some whole language teachers fill their classrooms with logos to show students that *graphemes* can represent language and meaning.

M-m

magic time — Students go through a "magic time" in which they begin to learn what writing is and what it represents. *Skills-based* teachers would probably call that magic time "readiness." "He's ten years old and still in magic time — that's why he's not reading yet." (Heard in Toronto.)

management — Often called classroom management, this term refers to teachers' efforts to manage classroom activities so that students learn at their own level and with their needs and abilities being recognized and accomodated. Personal contact with students is maintained through **conferences**, during which teachers assess students' progress. Management also entails record-keeping of some kind, usually records of student progress. (See **conference log**.)

mature writing — Another term for standard writing. Mature writing contains correct spellings of words and standard punctuation. Most whole language teachers view the learning of mature writing as secondary to the production of meaning. (See also **writing development**.)

meaningful learning — Whole language teachers believe that students should be involved in what they consider to be meaningful learning. They object to students devoting time and effort to filling in blanks in workbooks, often known as **drill and kill** activities. Meaningful learning denotes student-centered, **integrated learning** activities.

miscues — When students read, they often say words that are different from those in the actual text. Ken Goodman calls these miscues, since they often show that students *are* comprehending text and understanding what they read. For instance, the reader who reads: "I am walking to my home after school" instead of: "I am walking to my house after school" is, in fact, comprehending. A miscue analysis is a procedure for looking at all the sources of information a reader uses while reading.

models — Theorists have proposed many different models to account for the processes that occur during reading. Whole language teachers seem to favor the "psycholinguistic" model suggested by Ken Goodman, which maintains that reading is a cognitive process whereby readers extract minimal visual cues to guess words on the basis of their knowledge of syntactic and semantic structures and world knowledge. As noted under **miscues**, the student who reads: "I am walking to my home" instead of: "I am walking to my house" isn't making an error, but is reading with meaning. In 1986 I suggested that it was illogical to assume that reading **models** have immediate practical classroom applications, and that the **research** community should formulate a model of reading **instruction** instead.

morphemes — Morphemes are units of language meaning. Free morphemes can stand alone (for example, *man*), while bound morphemes cannot. *Un*-man-*ly* contains two bound morphemes, *un* and *ly*.

multiple copy collections — Many school districts own multiple copies of books written for students. These are often used with small groups, especially interest groups.

N-n

networking — An electronic communications system that allows computer users to communicate with other users in other locations. Networking allows students and teachers to communicate with others over great distances. For many whole language teachers who feel estranged in their own schools, networking also means making contact with other whole language teachers, in *support groups*, for instance.

O-o

one of them — A term used by whole language teachers to describe students from traditional classrooms. It is also used by traditional teachers to refer to students from whole language backgrounds. "I just had one of them transfer into my classroom, and all he wants to do is write!" (Heard in Calgary.) "I just got one of them in my classroom and he's a real *wallbanger* — he cries every time I ask him to write!" (Heard in Los Angeles.) (See also *them, they*.)

oral language development — Talk is important in whole language classrooms. Oral language development includes students talking to each other about their reading, writing, spelling, and life experiences, and is part of *integrated learning*.

oral reading — Most whole language teachers are horrified at the prospect of having students read "round robin." Nevertheless, their students frequently read aloud, spontaneously, the things they have written. They read aloud in groups during *chiming in*, *chanting*, *choral reading* or *jazzing* time. Whole language teachers are also convinced that they themselves should read aloud to and with students as often as possible, in order to model good phrasing and intonation.

ownership — When students come to feel that they have a right to choose what they want to learn, they develop a proprietorial feeling over their learning, a feeling of real ownership. (See also *empowerment*.)

P-p

parent newsletter — It is extremely important for parents to know about and understand the whole language approaches and procedures involving their children so that they do not react negatively to the non-traditional activities they see. "That teacher never does correct spelling, she just lets the kids spell any word any way they want. They aren't learning anything in that classroom!" (Heard in San Francisco.)

part language — A term used by people who seem to have doubts about whole language. Normally it is used as a joke or a jest, as in: "Okay, if whole language teachers teach whole language, do traditional teachers teach part language?" (Various versions heard in Richmond, Chicago, Austin, Sacramento, Anaheim, Los Angeles, Clearwater, and other assorted locations.) Generally speaking, traditional and whole language teachers tend to dislike each other. The whole language teacher believes the traditionalist's viewpoint is narrow, limited, and focused on meaningless workbook activities. The traditional teacher, on the other hand, views the whole language teacher as the very incarnation of disorganization and carelessness, one who allows, even appears to encourage, noisy and disorganized classroom behavior. Sadly, neither side seems willing to accept the other, as neither seems willing to compromise. Could elements of both traditions not be valuable to students?

peer editing — Students read each other's written work, make suggestions for changes, and generally help their classmates improve their writing to bring it into publishable form. (See also *publishing*.) Butler (1989) described some training programs designed to help students become good peer editors.

pen-mates, pen-pals — Writers need real audiences. Pen-mates can be students in the same school at different grade levels, students at different schools in the same city, or students in schools in other cities, counties, states, provinces, or countries. Many whole language teachers involve their students in electronic mail so that they can write to students in different countries with great ease and in a short amount of time. (See also *networking, poor-man's networking*.)

personal dictionaries — Students are given booklets, divided into alphabetic sections, made of unlined paper and covered with construction paper. Each time they ask how to spell a word, they enter it in their own personal dictionary. Many whole language teachers ask students to consult their dictionaries before they ask how to spell a word. In some cases, they even refuse to give students spellings because they prefer that they discover spelling patterns independently. (See also *key words, word walls*.)

philosophy — (See *whole language philosophy*.)

phonemes — The basic units of sound in a language. The word *but* begins with the phoneme /b/. *Phonics* is the study of the relationship between *graphemes* (letters) and phonemes (sounds).

phonetics — The study of speech sounds. Phonetics and *phonics* are often confused. Teachers do not normally teach phonetics. "Our students would learn to read better if teachers stopped teaching phonetics and started teaching whole language." (Comment by the chairman of the Vancouver School Board, reported in *The Vancouver Sun*.) Phonetics has little to do with the study of letters and the sounds they represent.

phonic generalization — A statement that tells about a relationship that exists between letters (*graphemes*) and sounds (*phonemes*). These statements are generalizations because there are often more exceptions to the rule than items that follow the rule, as in: "When two vowels go walking, the first one does the talking." Clymer (1963) found that this generalization, which describes the method for pronouncing the word *road*, had about 45% accuracy in predicting the pronunciation of words in first grade reading texts. Whole language teachers generally do not believe in directly teaching phonic relationships, and, in fact, Shapiro and I (1988) found that students learn phonic relationships by writing, without direct instruction.

phonic rule — Phonic rules describe the regular relationships existing between letters and sounds. However, since there are so many exceptions, the more accurate term used is ***phonic generalization***.

phonication, phonicating — ***Basals*** are designed to teach students letter-sound correspondences. They learn, for instance, to produce the sounds associated with letters, and then put the sounds together to form words. *C-A-T* is read *kuh-aaa-t, kuh-aaa-t, cat!* Phonication is painful to the listener and even more so to the reader, as he plows laboriously through the text producing sounds for each letter, often at a complete loss of understanding of the meaning of what he is "reading." "Students should be taught to read, not to phonicate." (Dr. Jerome Harste, University of Indiana.)

phonics — Phonics is the study of the relationships between letters (***graphemes***) and sounds (***phonemes***).

phonic writing — The stage in ***writing development*** when students invent spellings based on their growing knowledge of the relationship between letters and sounds.

picture writing — The stage in ***writing development*** at which students equate pictures with writing.

poor-man's networking — Some schools or school districts cannot afford the equipment or the phone rentals essential to networking. They send computer floppy disks through the mail. The major drawback is that they take the same time as regular mail to arrive. Floppy disks do, however, allow many students to write letters and capture them all on one small diskette.

predictable books — Predictable books, sometimes called pattern books, have patterns that students are easily able to perceive and use to read the texts. (See also ***wordless picture books***.)

prediction — An important part of reading and understanding is prediction. Whole language teachers are convinced that readers make predictions as they read, and they try to develop their students' ability to do this (see **DRTA**). Intermediate teachers often use activities that ask students to make predictions before they read. The procedure helps students comprehend the content of academic texts. (See my chapter in Froese, 1989.)

pre-phonetic — The stage in *writing development*, identified by Mayling Chow (1986), at which students produce text containing letters and numbers, but do not yet realize that letters represent sounds.

pre-phonic writing — Shapiro and I (1987) changed the term *pre-phonetic* to *pre-phonic*. Because they do not understand that there is a phonic relationship between letters and sounds, students write numbers and letter-like shapes that bear little relationship to what they say they have written. (See also *writing development*.)

print rich environment — Whole language teachers are convinced that students should be immersed in print. The most successful students in language arts are generally those from homes in which newspapers, magazines, books, and other reading materials are available, are esteemed, and are used and *seen* to be used. Whole language classrooms are also print rich environments.

process — The *traditional teaching* of language arts activities has focused on *product* rather than process. Students' writing and reading are measured and judged to be "good" or "poor." Whole language teachers view the language arts as manifestations of "thinking" — that is, as processes rather than products. Their literacy programs focus on process and place less emphasis on product, in the belief that improved products will result from programs that focus on process. (See also *reading process, spelling process, writing process*.)

product — The goal of a literacy program should be to produce students able to read, write, and spell well — in other words, capable of producing a good product. Most whole language teachers believe that this traditional view does not focus on the language arts as thinking *process*. (See also *reading process, spelling process, writing process*.)

publishing — Whole language teachers are convinced that students should write for real rather than imaginary audiences, or strictly for the teacher (the usual audience for school writing). They ask students to write and polish so that the written *product* can be published and read by real people. The computer is most often used for this purpose, since a good word processing program can help students edit and make their work publishable. *FrEd Writer* is a simple (and free) word processing program suitable for elementary students, but it does not have a spelling check, and some whole language teachers believe a spelling check helps students develop spelling abilities. A fairly simple word processing program that does contain a spelling check is the *Bank Street Story Book*. On the other hand, some teachers believe spelling checks interfere with students' independent *writing development*.

Q-q

quiet time — The whole language classroom is normally filled with student talk. However, there are periods when teachers ask students to work quietly on reading or writing (see *uninterrupted sustained silent reading, uninterrupted sustained silent reading or writing, uninterrupted sustained silent writing*). The duration of quiet time varies from classroom to classroom, anywhere from 20 to 40 minutes, but it usually occurs at least once a day.

R-r

range — Range describes the difference between the achievement levels of the "lowest" and the "highest" student in the same class. Traditionally, teachers have grouped students in order to match instruction more closely to their students' abilities. Then, in effect, they have taught to the average in the group. Whole language teachers allow and encourage students to develop at their own rate. Ironically, this procedure, in and of itself, may increase the actual range in a class. Shapiro and I (1988) found some whole language students in a first grade classroom in Vancouver who wrote better than grade eight students. They came from widely diverse backgrounds, rich and poor, from homes where reading was an esteemed activity and from homes where it was held to be without any value. Our observations seemed to indicate that students do grow more in whole language classrooms than in traditional ones. So, instead of having the customary grade range of one to four, that whole language teacher actually had a range of one to eight.

rap-write — Some intermediate teachers reserve the last 10 or 15 minutes each day for students to write in their "rap-write" books. Students record what they have done during the day, reflect on their learning, indicate what they would like to learn, and generally tell teachers about their progress. Teachers respond in the rap-write books, with suggestions for further study, comments about students' interests, etc. The rap-write books serve to give the teacher information about students' progress, and also help with classroom *management*. "Rap" actually means talk.

readiness — A term used to refer to the *skills* some teachers believe students need to have mastered in order to begin reading. Many whole language teachers are convinced that readiness is actually an artifact of readiness testing. Readiness tests contain items requiring students to differentiate between letters, identify words beginning with the same letter, and match upper- and lower-case letters. Whole language teachers believe a student learns to read and write by reading and writing, not by "drawing circles around all the letters that are the same" in a workbook.

reading — A complex cognitive ability that allows individuals to understand and interpret written text. Most whole language teachers believe that reading is a process in which a reader visually monitors print, selects minimal visual cues, and makes predictions based on semantic, syntactic, and world knowledge. *Miscues*, cases in which what is read differs from what is in the print, often show that readers do make predictions. (See also *models*.)

reading process — The strategies students use for learning to read are the focus of whole language instruction. Students learn to read through the process of reading, not by studying *phonics*, since meaning is the compelling force. Acquiring meaning is more important than the ability to answer multiple choice questions.

reading-writing-thinking approach (RWTA) — This term is sometimes used as a substitute for "whole language" by teachers, schools, and school districts, because it does not have the negative political overtones that "whole language" has in many areas. Whole language's sometimes negative image arises from the fact that it is viewed by many as an approach to literacy *instruction* that is unstructured, unsupported, disorganized, and promulgated by wild-eyed whole language *groupies* who worship, with unswerving devotion, at the feet of certain educator-gurus. The problem is not made any easier, either, by the fact that whole language teachers are prone to challenge the views and opinions of others, believing that whole language is the *only* way to teach. (See *zealot*.)

real audience — The usual writing program involves students writing material for the teacher, usually assignments. *Meaningful learning* requires that students have real audiences to write for, including students in other classrooms or schools, parents, etc. But surely teachers can also be considered a real audience? My answer is this: how *can* a teacher be a real audience when all too often their only response is to "set the paper on fire" with red marks of disapproval, further embellishing the whole with censorious comments, exhortations to improve and admonitions to rewrite? A real audience, surely, responds to a writer's meaning and not to the spelling, grammar, handwriting or use of the third person singular!

real language — Whole language teachers believe students should learn in situations that use real language, language they hear and read in the real world, rather than the contrived language of *basal readers*.

recording progress — Since whole language teachers do not assign grades in the traditional fashion, they must be prepared to report on students' growth in other ways. Keeping dated copies of students' writing over the period of a school year provides a good record of progress, besides being an excellent diagnostic tool. Shapiro and I (1988) found that students' writing revealed both their abilities and their needs, as well as their progress over a year.

research — It is a basic article of faith among whole language teachers that there exists a great body of research to support their approach. There is research that observes the *writing development* of preschool students (see *emergent literacy*), and a great deal of theorizing by the researchers. However, there is little actual research observing whole language *instruction* in classrooms. Some is beginning to be conducted, but not enough for many whole language teachers to persist in making claims as in the following conversation I had with a teacher in Burnaby: "There is a lot of research behind whole language instruction, saying that whole language is better than basal programs." "What research do you know about?" "Oh, I don't really know the names of people, they just told us last week at an inservice class that there was lots of research."

retelling — A preferred holistic measurement of students' comprehension of discourse. There are several kinds of retelling:

• Oral retelling of something read. This indicates to a teacher how well the student has read and understood the story.

• Oral retelling of something heard. This is a measurement of the student's oral comprehension.

• Written retelling (often called *written recall*) of something heard or read.

risking — This term refers to both students and teachers taking a chance in their learning. Risking means one might not be successful in a particular learning situation. For example, a student might attempt to read an extremely difficult story, and in so doing risks failing. Risking is important because students must learn to have faith in their own abilities and not fear failure.

role playing — Students assume roles and act out parts of a story.

rug time — This period, normally taking place in a corner of the room covered by a rug, is one in which the whole class sits and listens to the teacher. This is most often the time when the teacher reads aloud, but it may also be the time when students share things with their classmates, such as favorite books or something they have written. In kindergarten, rug time may also indicate nap time.

S-s

SRA, SRA kit — This refers to an individualized reading kit published by Science Research Associates. It allows teachers to provide reading programs designed to meet the needs and abilities of all students in a class by providing stories and activities at multiple levels (see *individualization*). Whole language teachers generally believe that the concept of offering individualized programs is a good one, but they are at odds with the SRA approach because of its focus on *skills* instruction in comprehension exercises.

SSR — Sustained silent reading, a short form for *uninterrupted sustained silent reading*.

SSROW — Sustained silent reading or writing, a short form of *uninterrupted sustained silent reading or writing*.

SSW — Sustained silent writing, a short form for *uninterrupted sustained silent writing*.

schema theory — Human beings, it is suggested, perceive the world in terms of schemata, overall "outlines" of objects, places, and events. A reader comprehends a text, it is thought, by applying the appropriate schema. Developing schemata is somewhat like developing background knowledge, and the best way to help students develop schemata is through real hands-on experience of the world (see *experiential*).

scope and sequence — Many teachers feel that reading is a complex of *skills* learned in a particular hierarchical order. A list of those skills, ordered according to difficulty, is called a scope and sequence chart, a document based on the notion that early skills form the basis of higher skills. The earliest skills are called *readiness* skills, and individuals cannot learn higher level skills until they have mastered these.

scripting — Some principals and teachers have attempted to establish methods for evaluating whole language classrooms. Scripting, which involves recording everything said in a classroom over a set period of time, is one. Normally, the principal is the one who does the scripting, which is then analyzed and discussed with the teacher.

semi-phonetic writing — An early stage in *writing development* in which students produce text which is beginning to have some relationship to language. Usually they use the capital letter representing the initial *phoneme* in a word to represent the word; for example, *D* represents *Daddy*. (See also *semi-phonic writing*, *phonics*.)

semi-phonic writing — Similar to semi-phonetic. Students produce text that shows they have begun to associate particular *phonemes* with particular letters.

sharing — Interesting writing done by students, and interesting books read by them, should be shared with other students. Whole language teachers themselves regularly share with their students things they have written. Usually, sharing takes place when the class is assembled as a group, often at *rug time*, and may be on an individual or a class basis. Many whole language teachers prefer the term sharing to the traditional "show and tell" because it is more "cooperative." (Comment made in Philadelphia.)

skills — The traditional view of teaching is that students must learn a series of skills that have been identified by teachers or, more likely, by textbook authors. Many *traditional teachers* view with suspicion those whole language peers who do not directly teach skills because they are convinced the skills are meaningless and, worst of all, that they focus students' attention on surface structures rather than meaning. "I don't know how kids are going to learn to read if their teachers don't teach them any skills. Didn't Van Cliburn have to practice thousands of scales before he played his first piece?" (Heard in Vancouver.)

skills-based — Many individuals are convinced that reading is a series of *skills* taught in a particular sequence (see *scope and sequence*). Teaching students the myriad of skills deemed important in learning to read is referred to as skills-based instruction.

spelling process — The view of *traditional teaching* is that students should come to be good spellers, that they should produce a good *product*. Most whole language teachers are convinced that, in spelling, the process is more important than the product. Students come to learn spelling relationships by taking risks and experimenting (see *risking*), and by using *invented spelling*, based on their growing knowledge of the relationships between letters and sounds, developed through real language activities.

stagic — ". . . the magic to reach and touch the stars of hope in a child's mind." (Cochrane, Cochrane, Scalena and Buchanan, page 142.) The authors state that "stagic" is composed of three elements: love, belief in children's ability to succeed, and knowledge of the *reading process* and of writing and spelling.

strategies — While most whole language teachers do not teach *skills*, they are anxious for their students to learn strategies, ways or methods for effective learning. They are also convinced that they should help their students to acquire *thinking* strategies.

students — A term used by secondary or upper elementary teachers to refer to the children in their classes. When speaking to teachers, one can judge whether or not they teach primary or older students by whether they use the term students or *children*. "My students are working on projects" versus "My children are working on projects."

support groups — Whole language teachers often feel estranged from their fellow teachers who teach in the traditional fashion. Some may even feel ostracized. To conquer feelings of loneliness, many have formed support groups to provide the opportunities to meet other whole language teachers who can offer encouragement and support. Support groups are formed through *networking*, and may be local or regional.

T-t

talk talk — A term referring to the content of normal oral discourse. The way people talk is different from the way books are written. Books generally contain *book talk*, unless of course it's *basalese*, which is entirely different from both talk talk and book talk. It is a language complete and sufficient unto itself.

TAWL — An acronym for Teachers Applying Whole Language. The term is often applied to organizations that support whole language teachers. (See also *support groups, TOWL*.)

them — A term referring to any teachers who have a different perspective on teaching and learning from that of the speaker. "Them" can, therefore, refer to either whole language or *traditional teachers*, depending upon who happens to be using it. (See also *one of them, they*.)

theme books, theme writing — Many whole language teachers suggest themes to their students, who then write stories which are stapled into theme books. These books, used as part of the reading program, may also be produced as **big books**.

theory — Many teachers have adopted the whole language approach because they feel there is **research** — usually invoked as "a great body of cognitive research that shows . . . " (see **they**) — supporting their teaching strategies. Unfortunately, there is little actual classroom research investigating whole language instruction, and most of the putative research cited consists of theorists' notions of what literacy learning and training involve.

they — A term referring to any teachers having a different perspective on teaching and learning from one's own. "They" can refer to either whole language teachers or **traditional teachers**, depending upon who uses the term (see **one of them**, **them**). It is also a term used by individuals to refer to researchers, as in: "They say there is good research to support whole language" or "They say students miss out on phonics in whole language classrooms." When asked for the source of this information or the identity of "they," the individuals making such claims are, usually, found to be resorting to hearsay evidence.

thinking — Whole language teachers are convinced that developing the ability to think is the ultimate goal of education. Not only that, they are convinced that reading and writing are important ways of developing that ability.

TOWL — An acronym for Teachers of Whole Language, teachers who seek each other out for mutual support (see **support groups**). TOWL is a version of **TAWL**, used primarily in the western United States and Canada. It is difficult to ascertain which groups came first, TAWL or TOWL. Many are simply called "whole language support groups."

trade books — Often used as a term to describe library books — in other words, books students will enjoy reading — as opposed to **basal readers**.

traditional classrooms, traditional teachers, traditional teaching — Traditional classrooms are considered by most whole language teachers to be formal, teacher-directed, and concentrated on teaching students *skills*. Most traditional teachers, it is thought, demand that their students be quiet and orderly while engaged in the task of completing worksheets and workbooks and the memorization of facts. Some people believe that traditional teaching also means that *basal readers* are used in the process. Whole language teachers sometimes use the term in a negative way, as in: "Poor child, he's the product of a traditional classroom." (Heard in Glendale.) The transition from a traditional to a whole language classroom can be quite difficult for both students and teacher. Only time will provide us with an answer to the question whether that kind of transition is possible. What will happen, for instance, when a grade four teacher gets students who readily write 40 page essays and, moreover, do so with ease?

transitional writing — A stage in the development of writing skills in which the student begins to produce standard spellings and sentences. However, it also contains many elements of *phonetic writing*, or *phonic writing*.

U-u

uninterrupted sustained silent reading (USSR) — Modeling is important for teachers. They must be seen by their students in the act of reading and, moreover, *enjoying* their reading. During USSR everyone, including teachers, reads silently, usually for about 20 minutes every day. The teachers' role in this is absolutely vital: to be seen reading. If they choose, instead, to correct papers, then they fail as *models* and USSR will be a waste of time. When USSR time is over, teachers must take the time to tell students about what they have been reading and, of course, to try to engage the students in discussions of *their* reading.

uninterrupted sustained silent reading or writing (USSRW) — Some whole language teachers allow their students either to read silently, as in *USSR*, or to write silently, as in *USSW*, depending upon their preferences. Also known as USSROW.

uninterrupted sustained silent writing (USSW) — Teachers are important as *models* for developing enthusiastic writers. During USSW, teachers should be seen enjoying writing. After USSW, if they think they have written something especially good, they should share the results, encouraging students to do the same. *Everyone, including the teacher*, writes during USSW.

V-v

valuing — Students and teachers in whole language classes learn to have positive *attitudes* toward writing and reading activities. "Valuing" refers to the act of appreciating language arts activities for their own value. "He's been valuing writing since he was in kindergarten." (Heard in San Diego.)

visualizing — Students are asked to visualize a scene in their heads before they write a story (see also *dreamin'*). This allows them to "see" characters and events before actually having to put pen to paper.

vocabulary — Many *traditional teachers* and critics of *whole language instruction* suggest that students will not learn to read important items of vocabulary. Shapiro and I (1988) found that students in whole language classrooms independently produced in their writing all of the high frequency vocabulary to which they would normally have been introduced in common *basal readers*.

W-w

wallbanger — A term referring to a hyperactive child who cannot be still for long. It may also refer to a student from a *traditional classroom* who transfers into a whole language classroom and objects to the new kinds of activities required. The term comes from the fact that these students often "get sent to the office for counseling," where they sit on chairs which they often tilt back and literally bang against the walls. (Heard in Austin.) On the other hand, sometimes it refers to a student from a whole language classroom who transfers into a traditional classroom and objects to the activities required. Both whole language teachers and traditional teachers refer to students transferring into their classrooms from different backgrounds as wallbangers, *them*, *one of them*, or *they*, as in: "They (whole language students) don't know how to do anything but sit and talk." (Heard in Abbotsford.)

webbing, semantic webbing — A method for visually representing the association of words. Semantic webbing is used to develop students' *thinking* abilities and to learn new vocabulary by associating known words to new words. "My sister's been doing whole language for three years. Her basic approach is to do semantic webbing for everything." (Heard in Clearwater.)

whole class instruction — Some whole language teachers believe that only the class as a whole should be taught. These teachers do not believe in *grouping* students, maintaining that grouping tends to lead to permanent groups that isolate and label students forever. Students are either taught individually or as a whole class.

whole-language — Froese (1989) suggested that the term *whole language* should be *whole-language* to represent its underlying meaning, which is one of unity. The language arts of listening, speaking, reading, and writing are manifestations of the same unified language ability. Grouping them together and using the term *whole-language* signals that underlying unity.

whole language basals — Publishing companies and textbook authors, sensitive to the negative criticism accruing to *basal readers*, have begun to produce basal series that have more natural language and contain more interesting materials. Many whole language teachers view the term with some derision. Teachers in many school districts, having been informed that "the district will become whole language," have opted for the comfortable reassurance of having whole language basals in their classrooms. To the purists among both groups, these hybrid series are anathema.

whole language instruction — The term whole language is wonderfully indefinable. Indeed, whole language teachers themselves have different definitions and viewpoints and, therefore, there are as many manifestations of whole language instruction as there are whole language teachers. However, since this is a volume filled with definitions and explanations, whole language instruction is:

- Teaching students to read whole stories rather than words.
- Having students read material that contains real language, not the contrived language of *basal readers*.
- Having students write from the very first day of school.
- Integrating all the language arts so that they do not become isolated and compartmentalized.
- Encouraging students to communicate with others in writing and speech.
- Fostering a love of reading and writing in students.
- Providing *models* of language use for students.
- Using good children's literature as part of the program.
- Encouraging students to grow through experimenting with text and *risking* in their learning.
- Encouraging literacy independence.
- Focusing learning on process rather than product.

whole language philosophy — Many whole language teachers believe their instructional programs are based on a philosophy. This is technically incorrect. Rather, it is based on teachers' beliefs about language learning. In actual fact, it may be more exact to say that whole language is based on a model of language learning that is, itself, based on extrapolating classroom strategies from *research* studies of preschool students in non-classroom settings.

wholes — Many whole language teachers believe human beings learn wholes rather than parts, and that students learn whole words better than they do letters. In fact, whole language teachers teach students to read whole stories, often by rote. Interestingly, this is not a particularly new approach: Jacotot, in 1823, was convinced that students would learn to read if they were given "whole" books. Students therefore memorized entire books, and the teacher's first job was to read the book aloud while the students listened.

wholistic — Many whole language advocates prefer the term *wholistic* to *holistic* because it more clearly delineates their belief in the importance of wholes.

word-by-word reading — Often known as "first-grade reading." Students read slowly, enunciating each word carefully, and in doing so, lose the meanings associated with phrases and clauses. Also referred to as "one-to-one eye-voice span constant" — which means that the reader's eye span (that is, what is absorbed visually) is a single word at a time. Mature readers, depending upon the material being read, are able to perceive five to nine words in a single eye fixation. Whole language teachers are convinced that *basals* focus students' attention on individual words and tend to turn them into word-by-word readers.

wordless picture books — Books containing illustrations but no written text. Teachers ask students to tell stories to accompany the texts. Usually wordless picture books are also highly *predictable books*.

word walls — Word walls are an alternative to *key words* and *personal dictionaries*. Students ask the teacher to spell words, which are put on flashcards and then stapled to the wall. In this case, students check the wall before they ask for help in spelling. One teacher in San Francisco had a "word room" with all walls and the ceiling covered with words! Some whole language teachers object to providing students with correct spelling, preferring them to learn spelling conventions independently.

writing development — In whole language, writing is not considered to be separate from the other language arts, and the traditional belief that students should become readers before they can be writers is scoffed at as outlandish. (See *readiness*.) Researchers have observed individual children in environments where literacy and literacy activities are highly valued producing letters and letter-like forms spontaneously. There seems to be a developmental sequence in preschool spontaneous writing development: scribbling (with meaning), perceiving print and drawing as synonymous, representing things with individual letters, writing initial consonants to represent words beginning with particular sounds, spacing between words, representing sounds with letters, inventing spellings, and producing the mature conventions of spelling and writing (DeFord, 1980; Dyson, 1981; Ferreiro, 1986; Hipple, 1985; Sulzby, 1986).

Variations in whole language classrooms produce different stages in students' writing development (see also *instruction*):

Implicit modeling means that teachers expect students to develop writing skills entirely independently. Mayling Chow (1986) found that when teachers provided implicit models, students' writing revealed five stages: the pre-phonetic, the semi-phonetic, the phonetic, the transitional, and the conventional or mature.

- In the ***pre-phonetic*** stage, writers produce letters or letter-like shapes. They do not understand, however, that letters correspond with sounds or words. They read the texts they create, but the reading varies over time. They use a small number of capital letters and numbers to write.

- In ***semi-phonetic writing***, the writers use letters to represent words or parts of words. They have begun to understand that there is a relationship between letters and sounds, but their words are often represented by single letters only, usually the letter corresponding with the first sound of the word — for example, *D* for *Daddy*. Chow referred to this phenomenon as making "phonetic hits." In our 1988 book, Shapiro, Froese and I called them instead "phonic hits," meaning that those students are beginning to associate particular ***phonemes*** of English with particular letters, and to learn phonic relationships.

- The *phonetic* writer knows that letters represent sounds, knows many correspondences, and is beginning to separate letters into word units. The phonetic writer relies on knowledge of the relationship between letters and sounds to spell words, sometimes using ***invented spelling***.

- In the ***transitional writing*** stage, writers begin to process words as visual units. Although the writing contains many invented spellings, it also contains many conventional, non-regular, spelling patterns.

- The *mature* writer knows many writing conventions, including "correct" spellings, and expends less energy on the mechanics of writing than writers in the other categories.

Explicit modeling means that teachers write on students' work comments containing the essence of what the students have written. These teachers begin the school year by asking students to write. If the students indicate they cannot write, the teacher asks what they would *like* to write if they could, and provides the written version in the student's book. This is the ***language experience approach***. In our 1988 study, Shapiro and I found that students whose teachers provided explicit models did not exhibit the stages mentioned above. Instead, within a month or so, all of the students had become transitional writers. It would seem that the teachers' writing models accelerated the students' writing development. We adapted Chow's categories, changing the terms, to reflect phonic knowledge, to *pre-phonic writing*, *semi-phonic writing*, and *phonic writing*.

writing process — Students' attention is focused on the *process* of writing rather than the *product* which, in *traditional classrooms*, is corrected with much attention to surface structure errors. Such a focus diverts attention from meaning and often makes students reticent to write. Emphasizing process helps students focus on meaning. (See also *reading process, spelling process*.)

X-x

x — I am sorry to say that I have failed to find any x or x-rated vocabulary. If you happen to encounter any, please let me know.

Y-y

yours — Whole language teachers want to develop students' *ownership* of their work (see also *empowerment*), and *yours* is a term used to indicate ownership. "This is good, and you must be happy because it's yours." (Heard in Oroville.)

Z-z

zealot — Many whole language teachers believe in their teaching to the point where they become intolerant whole language evangelists, often convinced that other teachers who are not of the same faith are doing something evil. "Those whole language people are such zealots that they are their own worst enemies." (Heard in Dallas.) Whole language teachers care so deeply about their students that it is particularly sad when some of them let their zeal render them fanatical, impatient with and censorious of their colleagues.

Contributor's Form

To: Lee Gunderson
University of British Columbia
2125 Main Mall
Vancouver
British Columbia V6T 1Z5

The term _____
is a new term ❑ not found in *A Whole Language Primer* / an
alternative definition ❑ for a term found there.

I give permission for Lee Gunderson to use the term and its
definition in future editions of *A Whole Language Primer*. I would ❑
like / would not ❑ like to be cited.

My name, title and address are:

_____

_____

_____

_____

_____   _____
Signature   Date

(Please provide as much information as you can, either on the back
of your photocopy of this form or, if you prefer, in an accompanying
letter, defining/redefining the term, describing the situation in which it
is commonly used, and stating where you heard it.)

Bibliography

Bank Street Story Book. New York: Mindscape, version 4, 1984.

Bormuth, John. "Comparable Cloze and Multiple Choice Comprehension Test Scores." *Journal of Reading,* vol. 10, 1967, pp. 291-299.

Butler, Sydney. "Writing." In V. Froese (Ed.) *Whole-Language Instruction: Theory and Practice.* Toronto: Prentice-Hall Canada Inc., 1989.

Chow, Mayling. "Nurturing the Growth of Writing in the Kindergarten and Grade One Years: How are the ESL Children Doing?" *TESL Canada Journal,* 1986, vol. 4, no. 1, pp. 35-47.

Clymer, Theodore. "The Utility of Forty-Five Phonic Generalizations." *The Reading Teacher,* 1963, vol. 16, pp. 252-258.

Cochrane, Orin, Donna Cochrane, Sharon Scalena and Ethel Buchanan. *Reading, Writing and Caring.* Winnipeg, Manitoba: Whole Language Consultants Ltd., 1984.

De Ford, Diane E. "Young Children and Their Writing." *Theory into Practice,* vol. 19, 1980, pp. 157-162.

Dyson, Anne H. "Oral Language: The Rooting System for Learning to Write." *Language Arts,* vol. 58, 1981, pp. 776-784.

Ferreiro, Emilia. "The Interplay between Information and Assimilation in Beginning Literacy." In W. H. Teale & E. Sulzby (Eds.) *Emergent Literacy: Writing and Reading.* Norwood, NJ: Ablex, 1986, pp. 15-49.

Froese, Victor. In V. Froese (Ed.) *Whole-Language Instruction: Theory and Practice.* Toronto: Prentice-Hall Canada Inc., 1989.

Goodman, Kenneth. In H. Singer & R.B. Ruddell (Eds.) *Theoretical Models in Reading.* Newark, Delaware: The International Reading Association, 1976.

Goodman, Kenneth. "A Linguistic Study of Cues and Miscues in Reading." *Elementary English,* 1965, vol. 42, pp. 639-643.

Gunderson, Lee. "Using Directed Reading-Thinking Activity (DRTA) to Improve Comprehension." *Prime Areas,* 1983, vol. 26, no. 2, pp. 9-12.

Gunderson, Lee. "An Epistemological Analysis of Word Recognition." *Reading-Canada-Lecture,* 1986, vol. 4, No. 4, pp. 247-254.

Gunderson, Lee & Shapiro, Jon. "Some Preliminary Findings on Whole Language Instruction." *Reading-Canada-Lecture,* vol. 5, 1987, pp. 22-26.

Gunderson, Lee & Shapiro, Jon. "Whole Language Instruction: Writing in 1st Grade." *The Reading Teacher,* vol. 41 (January 1988), pp. 430-437.

Gunderson, Lee, Jon Shapiro and Victor Froese. "Developmental Differences in Primary Writing Due to Teachers' Beliefs in Modeling Writing." Paper presented at the Thirteenth Annual Washington Organization of Research Development, Seattle, Washington, March 1988.

Hipple, Marjorie. "Journal Writing in Kindergarten." *Language Arts,* vol. 62, 1985, pp. 255-261.

Jacotot, Jean J. As cited in Fechner, Heinrich. *Grundriss der Geschichte der wichtigsten Leselehrarten.* Berlin, 1884.

Jones, Margaret B. and Edna C. Pikulski. "Cloze for the Classroom." *Journal of Reading,* vol. 17, 1974, pp. 432-438.

Rankin, Earl F. and Joseph W. Culhane. "Comparable Cloze and Multiple-Choice Comprehension Scores." *Journal of Reading,* vol. 13, 1969, pp. 193-198.

Robinson, Francis. *SRA Reading Laboratory.* Chicago: Science Research Associates, Kit 1B, 1971. (Various kits have different copyright dates.)

Rogers, Al. *FrEd Writer* V. 4, Hands On Training Company, 4021 Allen School Road, Bonita, California, 92002.

Shapiro, Jon. "When Do Boys Begin to Reject Reading as a Gender Appropriate Activity?" Paper presented at the National Reading Conference, San Diego, California, 1985.

Shapiro, Jon.. "Attitudes and Conceptions of Reading." Paper presented at the Eleventh Annual Reading Research Conference of the Washington Organization for Reading Development. Bellevue, Washington, 1986.

Shapiro, Jon. "Making Choices: Whole Language versus Traditional Reading Instruction." Keynote address, Second Annual Summer Literacy Institute, State University of New York, Genesee, New York, 1987.

Shapiro, Jon and Lee Gunderson. "A Comparison of Vocabulary Generated by Grade 1 Students in Whole Language Classrooms and Basal Reader Vocabulary." *Reading Research and Instruction,* vol. 27, 1988 (Winter), pp. 40-46.

Stauffer, Russell. "Slave, Puppet or Teacher?" *The Reading Teacher,* vol. 25, 1971, pp. 24-29.

Sulzby, Elizabeth. In W. H. Teale and E. Sulzby (Eds.) *Emergent Literacy: Writing and Reading.* Norwood, NJ: Ablex, 1986, pp. 15-49.

Taylor, Wilson L. "Cloze Procedure: A New Tool for Measuring Readability." *Journalism Quarterly,* vol. 30, 1953, pp. 415-433.